MW00440154

CAMS Examination Practice Test One

by

M. C. Maltempo, CAMS, CFE

MONEY COMPLIANCE PRESS
Published by VMJ Publishing
Ventures of MJ LLC
1848 2nd Ave
New York, NY 10128
USA

moneycompliance.com

Copyrights © 2016 by M. C. Maltempo

All rights reserved. No part of this book may be reproduced in any form or by any electronic or mechanical means, including information storage and retrieval systems, without permission in writing from the publisher, except by a reviewer, who may quote brief passages in a review.

FIRST EDITION

Library of Congress Control Number: TXu 2-002-064
Maltempo, M. C., 1980-
CAMS Examination Practice Test One
ISBN 978-0-9975335-0-7
1.   Anti-Money Laundering-Nonfiction.
2.   Test Preparation-Nonfiction.
3.   Professional Accreditation-Nonfiction.
1.   Title.
2016

Printed in the United States of America
1 2 3 4 5 6 7 8 9 10

CAMS Examination Practice Test One

by

M. C. Maltempo, CAMS, CFE

TABLE OF CONTENTS

FOREWORD

The *Certified Anti-Money Laundering Specialist Certification* is one of the most sought after credentials in financial services today. By choosing to take the exam, you are embarking on the quest to acquire one of the three criteria required to be designated with this industry standard of excellence. (Other two criteria are Education and Experience. See ACAMS website for more details.)

In 2015, the **Association of Certified Anti-Money Laundering Specialists** created two advanced credentials as well: CAMS-Audit and CAMS-FCI (Financial Crimes Investigations). In order to acquire these certificates, the candidate must have already acquired the CAMS designation by meeting all three criteria and approved by the Association.

When you register for the Exam, ACAMS sends you a 400-page study guide, which includes 100 test preparation questions. At the end of each chapter, there are several review questions as well. Approximately there are 120 questions available for you. Not all of the questions will be in the format of the Exam.

If you are reading this, you might be thinking that those questions were not enough. And you are not alone. I was a little surprised by the differences between the review questions and the questions in the Exam. Although I nearly aced the exam, the differences in the questions and answers made me believe that the study materials are enough to pass the exam but it isn't enough to get a perfect score without luck. That inspired me to develop the material in this book to help others. No one should have to rely on luck to pass an exam. As of this publication, about 75% of all test takers, including retest takers, pass the exam. As with many professional standards, the exam probably has a 40% pass rate for the first time test taker, though this is not confirmed. However, I don't believe that this is low pass rate is a result of difficulty but because of the inadequacy of the preparation materials, particularly the practice questions.

The *CAMS Examination Practice Test* by VMJ Publishing is here to help. The questions within this book are design to test your knowledge beyond the official study guide to prepare you more adequately for the exam.

Please note, this practice test does not replace the need to study the official study guide.

ABOUT THE BOOK

The **CAMS Examination Practice Test Two** is not a comprehensive study guide. Therefore, it should not be used as a sole source of material for preparation. It does, however, concentrate on what the official study guide is lacking: practice questions. Because the Exam is 120 question from a test bank ten times that size, it is important to try to cover both the most probably questions as well as the breadth of question types and subject matter of the Exam. In doing so, this book contains questions that may be more difficult than the actual exam. The idea here is that if you can do well in these practice tests, it is a good indicator that you will do well in the actual exam.

As with the official guide, you should aim to score the highest score possible. Unlike the official guide, if you get a passing score on these tests, it is more likely you will pass the Exam. But in order for that to be true, you have to be honest with yourself about the questions you answered correctly and the questions you guessed correctly. In your studies, you should aim to answer all questions correctly without guessing. To help you achieve this, the test is provided to you in two versions. The questions and the answers are the same, however, their orders are different. It is highly recommended that the after reviewing the official study guide and the questions provided therein, you should attempt at version one of the practice test. Afterward, take at least a day to review the materials again before tackling version two.

As with any exam preparation material, this book makes no guarantees that you will do well. You will get as much as your effort and talents allow. You cannot do much about your natural talents, but you can control your effort. So, give it all you got.

HELPFUL TIPS

As you know by now, the exam is 120 multiple choice questions. You will be given 3.5 hours to complete the Exam. The exam is not designed to test your recall ability. It is designed to test your knowledge. For a native English speaker, the allotted time is more than adequate.

The average reading pace for a native English speaker is 200 words per minute. This rate is highly unlikely for 3.5 hours. You will probably average 150 words per minute. You have 1 minute 45 seconds per questions, and any question you answer more quickly will provide a time cushion with the remainder. At 150 words per minute, it will take you a whole minute to read the longest question-stem and answer-choices. This gives you at least 45 seconds to solve each question. Considering your

However, the multiple choice questions do not always mean there is just one answer. Some questions will ask you to select all of the correct answers, which may be more than one. And many questions are negative or inverted questions (e.g. "select from the following the activities that would **NOT** raise a red flag," emphasis will not be in the exam).

With all this said, I have compiled a short list of helpful tips about both studying the material and taking the exam.

STUDYING THE MATERIAL

A. **Be able to explain how to launder money to someone else.** Much of what you will be tested will not require you to solve problems; they will ask you to identify various ways money can be laundered. You must know the mechanics of money laundering so that the various methods tested will not throw you off.

B. **Spend most of your time studying Chapters Two, Three, and Four.** The exam mostly focuses on those chapters of the Official Study Guide.

C. **Remember the difference between the methods of money laundering and terrorist financing.** Money laundering is the methods of legitimatizing proceeds from illicit activity. Terrorism financing could be, and often is, funds from legitimate business activities.

D. **Overlook the relevance of the real world example in the Official Study Guide.** Surprisingly, the Official Study Guide is not written very well. It will give you examples from real life do not reflect the text you've just read. Still, they are a great way to develop your judgment on what to do in scenarios, which are tested. Study them but ignore how relevant they are to where they are presented to you.

E. **The Glossary is a great testing tool.** If are willing to be honest with yourself, try to be able to write a definition of each of the glossary terms in your own words and check them against the definition provided. In my assessment, the percentage you get correct in this exercise will best indicate how well you will do in the exam.

F. **Know your FATF's, UN's, Egmont's, Wolfberg's...** Knowing the unique roles of various NGO's is an important source of information for the compliance officer, so, the exam tests you on them.

G. **There are no trick questions.** So, don't waste your time thinking up test strategies. Either you know the material or you do not.

TAKING THE EXAM

A. Follow your instincts. The exam questions are not always written very well. Sometimes the pronouns do not match the subject of the sentence. Sometimes paragraphs are not written in parallel sentence construction. If you have studied the material, remain confident that your initial interpretation of the question is correct.

B. Take your time. You have 1 minute 45 seconds per question. The average reading pace for a native English speaker is 200 words per minute. This rate is highly unlikely for a duration of 3.5 hours. You will probably average 150 words per minute. Because you can accumulate the time you don't spend on an answer, you will accumulate extra time very quickly. At 150 words per minute, it will take you a whole minute to read the longest question-stem and answer-choices. This gives you at least 45 seconds to solve each question. Even the longest of them probably will not take you 45 seconds to solve. If these figures scare you, then let me help you ease the stress of time: Most questions-stems and answer-choices are 75 words in total. This means, most of the time, one average, you will accumulate no less than 30 seconds. By the end of the Exam, you may find yourself with nearly an hour of spare time.

C. Choose all of the correct answers. Unlike most multiple choice questions, the CAMS Exam questions often have more than one correct answer and you will be asked to choose all of them. You will really have to know your material in order to figure out if you must choose one, two, three or four correct answers.

D. Do not take a break unless it is absolutely necessary. You won't gain anything from a break. You will only increase any doubts you may have about how well you are doing. Just make sure to take a drink of water and go to the bathroom before you enter the exam room.

E. Do wear the earplugs. If earplugs are provided, wear them. Even if the facility is quiet, you will read faster when you are hearing your own voice reading the test insie your head.

F. Be confident but humble. This is not an exam you can ace without luck, but this is an exam you can definitely pass.

CAMS Examination Practice Test One

Version One

Question 1

Which of the following is cannot be a method of money laundering?

 A. Purchasing Structured Financial Products

 B. Cuckoo smurfing

 C. Payable Through Accounts

 D. Black Market Peso Exchange

Question 2

Which of the following is an indication of possible money laundering?

 A. An automobile insurance plan bought through an insurance agent.

 B. Redemption of bond at significant discount.

 C. Purchasing a mutual fund and individual stocks for a single account with a broker-dealer.

 D. A financial adviser selling a Credit Derivative Swap to an ambitious young professional opening an IRA.

Question 3

A method of laundering money through international trade is by...

       A. Do not invoice for goods

       B. Only over-invoicing of goods

       C. Only under-invoicing of goods

       D. Both, over- and under-invoicing of goods

Question 4

What is considered a beneficial owner of an account?

Person or Entity that...

       A. Is the person or entity on legal documents.

       B. Is ultimately entitled to the funds in the account.

       C. Will inherit the funds in the account at the death of the account holder.

       D. Is representing a client who has the claim to the funds.

Question 5

What activity is it when a depositor makes multiple deposits to evade the bank's reporting threshold?

> A. Layering
>
> B. Integrating
>
> C. Dividing
>
> D. Structuring

Question 6

What are the goals of AML Programs?

> A. Prevent and detect money laundering and terrorist financing.
>
> B. Satisfy regulatory requirements.
>
> C. Report suspicious activities to FinCEN or other proper authorities of a given jurisdiction.
>
> D. Provide training to employees about the detection, policies, and procedures pertaining to AML.

Question 7

How should the responsibility to comply be required?

       A. Make compliance a condition of employment.

       B. Make internal audit check for efficacy of the internal controls.

       C. Make employees swear an oath to compliance.

       D. Make compliance an option that is rewarded with bonuses.

Question 8

What should the compliance officer do after an appropriate regulatory investigator requests to interview the bank's employees?

       A. Seek the bank's counsel's advice regarding the necessity of a subpoena or a warrant.

       B. Ignore the request until a warrant or subpoena is presented.

       C. Call the employee's manager to require the employee to be interviewed.

       D. Seek the bank's counsel's advice regarding how to reject the request.

Question 9

Which of the following are not recommended procedures for filing STRs?

A. STRs should be centralized for review to ensure uniformity

B. STRs should be filed multiple times by each employee that comes across the activity.

C. STRs should only be filed after the suspicious actor has been notified.

D. STRs should only be filed after Legal has approved the filing.

Question 10

FBI provides a bank with a warrant requesting account information on the bank's customer, who is a known terrorist suspect. The bank should...

A. Provide the requested information after sending a notification to the customer.

B. Not provide the requested information until the customer has provided approval to the bank.

C. Provide the requested information.

D. Not provide the requested information.

Question 11

When a financial institution is responding to a formal criminal investigation by a law enforcement agency, what is the primary purpose of requiring information going through a central point within the institution?

    A. To be able to ensure that nothing damaging to the financial institution gets released.

    B. To ensure that responses are timely and thorough, and that privileged material is not inadvertently handed over.

    C. To ensure that the employees of the institution do not divulge information that would breach the privacy rights of customers.

    D. To ensure that there is one person who can adequately and thoroughly apprise the Board of Directors of the progress of the investigation.

Question 12

When should a financial institution consider retaining an experienced outside counsel to assist it?

    A. Whenever the institution receives a subpoena from any law enforcement agency.

    B. When the institution itself appears to be the target of a criminal investigation.

    C. When law enforcement appears to be focused on the accounts of a very good and long-standing customer of the institution.

    D. When the banking agencies criticize the adequacy of the institution's AML monitoring procedures.

Question 13

What are practical tips in interviewing employees with regard to an unusual or suspicious transaction that they have witnessed?

A. Interview the employees as soon after the occurrence as possible in order to ensure that their memories are fresh.

B. Put the employees at ease during the interview and start with relatively easy, non-controversial, questions before getting into more sensitive matters.

C. Use open-ended questions for the employees in order to ensure that the questions do not dictate what the expected answer is.

D. Control the interview as much as possible in order to attempt to resolve the matter quickly and uncover the wrongdoer.

Question 14

When a bank receives a subpoena, the bank should first...

A. Start its own investigation internally.

B. Begin a social media campaign to mitigate any negative consequences.

C. Sue the account holder that caused the subpoena in the amount of the total cost it took to response properly to the subpoena.

D. Immediately notify the Board of Directors.

Question 15

When a new customer immediately transfers the initial deposits to a foreign bank, the compliance officer should first...

      A. Start an investigation.

      B. File a preliminary STR or SAR.

      C. Contact the financial regulator of that jurisdiction.

      D. Notify the Board of Directors.

Question 16

You are a compliance officer. One of your bank's customers is a Paavo Jarvi, a jeweler in New York. He has setup an account to receive payments from sales. The records show that he used to receive wire transfers for all of his sales across the Unite States, but he started receiving transfers from a correspondent bank account under his own name. Which of the following are AML red flag?...

      A. The account he setup to receive his sales proceeds had transfers out to his personal checking account.

      B. The correspondent bank account in his own name suggest that he ismaking sales abroad but the payments origins are unknon.

      C. The correspondent bank account in his own name suggests that he is moving his business abroad.

      D. The account he setup to receive his sales proceeds never received real sales.

Question 17

How should a compliance officer initially respond to a law enforcement inquiry?

A. Resist cooperation so that there is documented evidence that the bank tried to protect its customers and employees.

B. Cooperate fully as much as the laws allow.

C. Cooperate after the law enforcement as agreed to a nondisclosure agreement.

D. Refer law enforcement to outside counsel.

Question 18

EU *Third Directive on the Prevention of the Use of the Financial System for the Purpose of Money Laundering and Terrorist Financing* applies to which of the following firms?

A. Auditors, estate agents based in the EU.

B. US Financial institutions covered by the USA PATRIOT Act.

C. Shell firms inside and outside the EU.

D. EU based high value good dealers who deal in cash of 10,000 Euro or more.

Question 19

Which of the following is the most difficult regulatory challenge facing a foreign financial institution with a correspondent banking relationship in the US?

> A. USA Patriot Act
>
> B. Base Due Diligence Principles for Banks
>
> C. FATF Guidance on Terrorist Financing
>
> D. UN Security Council Resolution on Correspondent Banking

Question 20

Which of the following should a national legislature consider when criminalizing money laundering in line with FATF 19 Recommendations?

> A. Do no limit the number of specific predicate offenses for money laundering.
>
> B. Criminalize conspiracy or association to engage in money laundering.
>
> C. Indicate whether it is relevant that a predicate offense may have been committed outside the local jurisdiction.
>
> D. Require money laundering offenses to prove that the offender has actual knowledge of a criminal connection to the funds.

Question 21

The FATF 40 Recommendations say that countries should...

      A. Not allow bearer shares and legal persons that are able to issue bearer shares.

      B. Gather statistics on STRs; prosecutions and convictions; and provide mutual legal assistance, but not necessarily on other international requests for cooperation.

      C. Consider the feasibility of a system where banks and other financial institutions and intermediaries would report currency transactions without indicating a minimum fixed amount.

      D. Not approve the establishment or accept the continued operation of shell banks.

Question 22

According to the FATF 40 Recommendations, "designated non-financial businesses and professionals" include...

      A. Casinos, real estate agents and dealers in precious stones.

      B. Money service businesses, a, gatekeepers, and issuers of electronic money.

      C. Dealers in precious metals, lawyers, commodity futures traders.

      D. Life insurance companies, real estate agents and notaries.

Question 23

FATF has consistently noted the use of casinos in money laundering schemes in its annual typologies reports. One laundering technique involving casinos is…

        A. Asking for winner's checks to be made out in the name of third persons or without a payee.

        B. Abusing casinos by circumventing its gatekeepers.

        C. Prepaying a casino token or chip by using funds that are already in the casino system, creating a debit balance.

        D. Extensive gambling via multiple games through the casino.

Question 24

In what year did the EU adopt the ***First Directive on Prevention of the Use of the Financial System for the Purpose of Money Laundering***

        A. 1988

        B. 1991

        C. 2001

        D. 2005

Question 25

In what year did the EU adopt the *Third Directive on Prevention of the Use of the Financial System for the Purpose of Money Laundering*

      A. 1988

      B. 1991

      C. 2001

      D. 2005

Question 26

How many recommendations are there in the *EU Third Directive on the Prevention of the Use of the Financial System for the Purpose of Money Laundering and Terrorist Financing*

      A. 40

      B. 28

      C. 16

      D. 13

Question 27

EU *Third Directive on the Prevention of the Use of the Financial System for the Purpose of Money Laundering and Terrorist Financing* applies to...

    A. Bankers

    B. Auditors

    C. Tax advisers

    D. Insurance brokers

Question 28

Which institution released the BSA/AML Examination Manual?

    A. FFIEC

    B. OCC

    C. FinCEN

    D. OFAC

Question 29

What is the primary risk on concentration accounts?

A. Additional recordkeeping is necessary and could be accidentally missed.

B. None, concentration accounts cannot be accessed by clients.

C. None, concentration accounts are a way to mitigate money laundering risk.

D. Customer identification could be separated from the transaction amounts.

Question 30

Which of the following are money laundering risks associated with Broker-Dealers?

A. Ease of converting currencies and financial products.

B. Brokerage firms provide anonymity from the market by being named nominee/trustee of client funds.

C. Commission-driven environment pressures broker-dealers to cut corners.

D. Speed of transactions.

Question 31

What is the risk associated with real estate industry?

A. High percentage of money laundering cases involves real estate.

B. Rural properties are ideal for growing and storing drugs.

C. Construction expenses are easily manipulated for purposes of laundering, especially when the launderer is the acting as contractor.

D. Broker's escrow accounts normally have large and diverse transactions taking place, making it ideal for laundering.

Question 32

What is the risk associated with prepaid credit/debit cards?

A. Like loans, it has an application process.

B. Like travelers checks, it requires signature.

C. Like checks, it has a definite associated identification.

D. Like cash, it can be anonymous.

Question 33

Which group is the most important to get buy-in when developing an AML Program?

> A. Senior Management
>
> B. Internal Audit
>
> C. IT
>
> D. Legal

Question 34

What would be the most effective way to keep senior management updated on the efficacy of the AML Program?

> A. Provide a report with metrics of the key elements of the program for a given period, compare it to a relevant period and against a stated measurable goal.
>
> B. Provide a report that shows how much money was spent on the AML Program.
>
> C. Provide a report of the number of SARs and STRs that have been filed.
>
> D. Provide a report describing a representative experience of an employee's involvement in the compliance program.

Question 35

In order to deter money laundering…

    A. Banks should have an internal secret police.

    B. Banks should encourage employees to snoop on each other.

    C. Banks should advertise ways to avert tax authorities.

    D. Banks should make a telephone hotline available to report activities anonymously.

Question 36

A money laundering risk associated with charities and non-profit organizations is…

    A. That these entities might have been created to evade taxes.

    B. That these entities are sometimes involved with the poor and the sick.

    C. That some of these entities run major sports leagues.

    D. That these entities might have been created specifically to launder money.

Question 37

What are the similarities between money laundering and terrorist financing?

A. Both activities are a result of religious association.

B. Both activities are originate in Latin America.

C. Both activities are originate in the Middle East.

D. Both activities could be a result of illicit activities.

Question 38

What is an Alternative Remittance System (ARS)?

A. A payment system at the Bank of International Settlements for government transactions.

B. A payment systems only for global corporations.

C. A software that allows for wire transfers without the use of banks.

D. A system of financial services provided by non-financial services firms, often in developing economies.

Question 39

What is Anti-Money Laundering International Database (AMLID)?

     A. A database of laws and regulations pertaining to money laundering at the US Department of Justice.

     B. An FBI database of law enforcement contacts in other jurisdictions.

     C. A database at FATF of suspected money launderers and their organizations.

     D. A database in the International Money Laundering Information Network at the UN Office on Drugs and Crime that contains laws, regulations, and analysis, as well as contact information for law law enforcement in various jurisdictions.

Question 40

What is International Money Laundering Information Network (IMoLIN)?

     A. A network of corporate governance, risk, and compliance professionals around the world.

     B. A division of Financial Crimes Enforcement Network (FinCEN).

     C. A network of best money launders where they can share best practices.

     D. An Internet-based network assisting governments, organizations and individuals in the fight against money laundering.

Question 41

What is Bank Secrecy Act?

A. 1972 US legislation that requires banks to maintain absolute secrecy about the identity of their clients.

B. An addendum to the 1930 Advisers Act

C. A major part of the USA PATRIOT Act of 2001

D. 1970 US legislation that requires reporting and recordkeeping at financial institutions.

Question 42

What is Bank Secrecy Act? Matthew Salesses is a new customer seeking life insurance products. Which of the following would an AML red flag?

A. He makes his wife his first beneficiary upon his death.

B. He makes full use of the free lookback period.

C. He takes a loss and ends the contract.

D. He reads the insurance contract carefully.

Question 43

What is a bare trust?

    A. A trust account that has little or no funds.

    B. A trust account where the ultimate beneficial owner must reveal all assets within to the government.

    C. A special trust in Sharia Law that allows lending of money to those within the family.

    D. A trust where the trustee has only one duty, which is to convey the trust assets to the named beneficiary at the appropriate time.

Question 44

What is a bearer share certificate?

    A. A corporate debt certificate that gives the right to convert it to equity shares at a certain share price.

    B. A corporate equity share certificate of a bank holding company.

    C. A corporate equity certificate that a shareholder can print from home or office.

    D. A corporate equity share certificate with its ownership given to the person holding it.

Question 45

What is a bureau de change?

        A. A special piece of furniture for metal coins.

        B. French exchange for commodities and currencies.

        C. Change Management Office of the Federal Government.

        D. A retail currency exchanger.

Question 46

What is a Bust-Out?

        A. A scheme to provide my to a company that needs funds for an expansion project but to write in covenants that make the financing of the expansion impossible

        B. A scheme to bankrupt a company in order to reorganize and agree with lenders to bust-out previous loans

        C. A scheme to infiltrate a money laundering network by providing them with the sales of fake drugs

        D. A scheme to run and hide with loan proceeds that are greater than the value of the borrower company or property, leaving lender to take a loss at bankruptcy.

Question 47

What is a Commission Rogatoire?

A. A formal request to the French National Government to perform an investigation at a local bank.

B. A document permitting foreign subjects to perform investigations at French banks.

C. An order by one government to another to provide legal or judicial assistance.

D. A formal request from one government to another government for legal or judicial assistance.

Question 48

What is cuckoo smurfing?

A. A method of hiding insider trading information (originally done inside photoshopped drawings of the Smurfs)

B. A method of corporate espionage where the spy is embedded for years inside of a bank to discover security weaknesses.

C. A scheme of paying an investor with the funds received by a newer investor and calling it an investment return.

D. An alternative remittance scheme that hides the transaction in an legitimate transaction of unrelated party, usually facilitated by a financial professional.

Question 49

What is a Currency Transaction Report (CTR)?

A. Report that documents the amount of currency transferred in and out of a bank in a given period.

B. Report that documents the amount of foreign currency transferred in and out of a bank in a given period.

C. Report that documents suspicious transactions.

D. Report that documents large currency transactions.

Question 50

CDD is the abbreviation for...

A. Duties

B. Core Data Dumps

C. Corporate Data Definitions

D. Customer Due Diligence

Question 51

What is a Downstream Correspondent Clearer?

    A. A correspondence bank that provides banking services to correspondence banking client.

    B. A clearing house for checks that were endorsed by the recipient to pay a secondary recipient.

    C. A clearing house within the US Postal Service that delivers certified government checks.

    D. A correspondence banking client that provides banking services to its own clients through the correspondence account.

Question 52

EFT is an abbreviation for...

    A. Exchange Funded Transfer

    B. Electronic Financial Transaction

    C. Electronic Fraud Transverse

    D. Electronic Funds Transfer

Question 53

What is an extradition?

      A. The act of transferring funds in the tradition of the local jurisdiction.

      B. The act of extracting identification of potential financing of terrorism.

      C. A method of corporate espionage where the spy is embedded for years inside of a bank to discover security weaknesses.

      D. Often requiring a treaty for it to take place, the act of surrendering a person by one country to another country.

Question 54

What is the mission of FATF?

      A. To administer and enforce economic and trade sanctions based on US foreign policy and national security goals.

      B. To review and grant special financing for defendants at the International Criminal Court in the Haag.

      C. To provide loans to developing countries for capital program

      D. To set standards and promote effective implementation of legal, regulatory and operational measures for combating money laundering and terrorist financing.

Question 55

FIU is an abbreviation for…

        A. Federation of Insurance Underwriters

        B. Federalist Interpretation Union

        C. Financial Intelligence United

        D. Financial Intelligence Unit

Question 56

What is a front company?

        A. A company that receives the revenues for tax purposes even though the products are sold by another company, both owned wholly by a third company.

        B. A company setup in a foreign jurisdiction with no corporate address or named executives or board members.

        C. A limited liability company that is owned by a publicly traded corporation.

        D. A legitimate business used as a vehicle for laundering money.

Question 57

What is a harmful or preferential tax regime?

> A. A country with very high taxes that makes business transactions expensive.
>
> B. A military controlled state that is enforcing a kleptocracy.
>
> C. A US state with low or no tax rate in order to attract business.
>
> D. A country with low or no tax rate in order to attract business.

Question 58

What is a hawala?

> A. A system of merchants that provide short-term financing for local businesses without the use of a letter of credit.
>
> B. A traditional Indian method of accounting that used tea leaves and sacks of saffron to keep a record of inventory being warehoused by a common warehouse.
>
> C. A system of merchant banks that provide fund transfers by using their ordinary trading business across borders.
>
> D. A system of merchants that provide fund transfers by using their ordinary trading business across borders.

Question 59

IVTS is an abbreviation for...

A. International Value Transfer System

B. International Value Taxation System

C. Informal Value Taxation System

D. Informal Value Transfer System

Question 60

What is International Narcotics Control Strategy Report?

A. Annual report on the state of drug trafficking and money laundering issued by the United Nations

B. Annual report on the efforts of the CDC to treat patients addicted to various illicit drugs

C. Biannual report on the state of drug trafficking and money laundering issued by the Office of the Chancellor of the Exchequer

D. Annual report on the state of drug trafficking and money laundering issued by the US Department of State.

Question 61

Placement

      A. First phase of money laundering with the goal of entering the legitimate financial system

      B. Second phase of money laundering with the goal of obfuscating the origin of the placed funds.

      C. Third phase of money laundering with the goal of using the laundered funds for a legitimate purpose.

      D. Fourth phase of money laundering with the goal of using legitimate funds for illegitimate purposes.

Question 62

Layering

      A. First phase of money laundering with the goal of entering the legitimate financial system

      B. Second phase of money laundering with the goal of obfuscating the origin of the placed funds.

      C. Third phase of money laundering with the goal of using the laundered funds for a legitimate purpose.

      D. Fourth phase of money laundering with the goal of using legitimate funds for illegitimate purposes.

Question 63

Integration

    A. First phase of money laundering with the goal of entering the legitimate financial system

    B. Second phase of money laundering with the goal of obfuscating the origin of the placed funds.

    C. Third phase of money laundering with the goal of using the laundered funds for a legitimate purpose.

    D. Fourth phase of money laundering with the goal of using legitimate funds for illegitimate purposes.

Question 64

What is the loan back method?

    A. A way to launder money by over-paying taxes and then to receive a refund later to receive a government check.

    B. A way to swap an existing loan with the bank for a new loan in order for the bank to record lower risk rating to cheat the Federal Reserve requirements.

    C. A way to provide mortgage loans to those who defaulted for the same house and same terms as the previous loan.

    D. A way to launder money by borrowing money and then paying back the money with the illicit funds.

Question 65

What is a lockbox?

      A. A box that can be used to store sensitive items in a bank vault.

      B. A box that holds the server location of all of the bank's client accounts.

      C. A service offered by banks where the bank will pay the invoices and withdrawal funds on behalf of the client.

      D. A service offered by banks where the bank will receive payments in a post office box and makes the deposits on behalf of the client.

Question 66

What is a Mock Trial on Money Laundering?

      A. A law school program sanctioned by the ABA and overseen by the DOJ to teach law students for a career in prosecution of financial crimes.

      B. A practice by the ICC to let each side practice their arguments against each other in order to refine application of laws.

      C. A program that helps FBI and DEA agents practice testifying in court on financial crimes prosecution.

      D. A joint program of the UNODC and CICAD that teaches governments how to investigate and prosecute crimes.

Question 67

MSB is an abbreviation for...

        A. Mortgage Service Business

        B. Money and Securities Business

        C. Money Sanctions Bank

        D. Money Services Business

Question 68

MLAT is an abbreviation for...

        A. Mutual Legal Action Treaty

        B. Mutual Legislative Action Treaty

        C. Mutual Legal Assistance Tax

        D. Mutual Legal Assistance Treaty

Question 69

What are Nostro Accounts?

A. Accounts for correspondence bank that provides banking services to correspondence banking client.

B. Accounts for correspondence banking client that receives banking services from a correspondence bank.

C. Accounts for the clients of correspondence banking client.

D. Accounts correspondent account for a foreign bank that provides a correspondent account for the domestic bank, a mutual correspondent bank.

Question 70

What is an offshore bank?

A. A alternative remiter that serves the underbanked in developing economies.

B. A bank that is not licensed to provide banking services in foreign currencies.

C. A bank that insures insurance companies for casualty insurance plans.

D. A bank that is not licensed to provide banking services in domestic currency.

Question 71

What is a payable through account?

A. A bank account opened by another bank on behalf of client in order evade disclosure rules.

B. A bank account opened by a non-bank client who seek to provide unlicensed banking services.

C. A bank account for a retail merchant just for paying business expenses.

D. A bank account opened by another bank on behalf of client in order for that client to receive banking services.

Question 72

What is a predicate crime?

A. Crimes are gambling with investor money in casinos rather than in the strategy laid out in the prospectus.

B. Crimes underlying legitimate business activity with illicit proceeds.

C. Money laundering or terrorist finance activity are predicate crimes.

D. Crimes underlying money laundering or terrorist finance activity.

Question 73

What is the Report on the Observance of Standards and Codes (ROSC)?

A. Report that summarizes the efforts of the OECD and ADB to implementing international AML and anti-graft standards

B. Report that summarizes the efforts of the World Bank and IMF to implementing international AML and anti-graft standards

C. Report that summarizes the efforts of the OECD and ADB to implementing international accounting and auditing standards

D. Report that summarizes the efforts of the World Bank and IMF to implementing international accounting and auditing standards

Question 74

What is retrospective due diligence?

A. Due diligence of the due diligence practices of the bank.

B. Due diligence of returning new customers.

C. Due diligence of closed accounts.

D. Due diligence performed on existing customers.

Question 75

What is an example of a Self Regulatory Organization?

    A. New York Stock Exchange

    B. American Bar Association

    C. American Institute of Certified Public Accountants

    D. FINRA

Question 76

What is Structuring?

    A. The practice of investing illicit funds in the capital markets to launder returns.

    B. The practice of executing financial transactions in a specific pattern calculated to trigger reporting rules

    C. The practice of investing legitimate funds in the Black Market Peso Exchange to launder returns.

    D. The practice of executing financial transactions in a specific pattern calculated to avoid reporting rules.

Question 77

SAR is an abbreviation for...

      A. Suspicious Adverse Report

      B. Suspended Activity Report

      C. Securitized Asset Report

      D. Suspicious Activity Report

Question 78

What is a typology?

      A. The methods of financing terrorism.

      B. The methods of financing front businesses.

      C. The methods of transporting narcotics.

      D. The methods of money laundering.

Question 79

Who are vital service providers?

    A. Accountants, architects, contractors, construction companies, civil engineers

    B. Accountants, attorneys, doctors, nurses, EMTs, police officers, firefighters

    C. Accountants, attorneys, government workers

    D. Accountants, attorneys, broker-dealers, financial institutions, telecommunications firms, and transportation companies

Question 80

What is the Wolfsberg Group?

    A. Group of 20 central bank governors that have agreed on a set of AML guidelines.

    B. Group of 24 developing countries that have agreed on a set of AML guidelines.

    C. Group of 7 Finance Ministers that have agreed on a set of AML guidelines.

    D. Group of 11 large banks that have agreed on a set of AML guidelines.

Question 81

What are the minimum requirements for an effective AML program?

        A. Written internal policies, procedures and controls

        B. Designated AML compliance officer

        C. On-going employee training

        D. Independent review to test the program

Question 82

What is the primary benefit advertised for Asset Protection Trusts (APTs)?

        A. EU trustees may not have to comply with US courts.

        B. US trustees may not have to comply with EU courts.

        C. Domestic trustees may not have to comply with US courts.

        D. Foreign trustees may not have to comply with US courts.

Question 83

CTR must be filed for currency activity including transactions greater than...

A. $25,000.00

B. $3,000.00

C. $7,000.00

D. $10,000.00

Question 84

What is a document that allows a financial institution to release customer information to an appropriate government investigator?

A. Customer Information Form

B. Customer Information Request

C. Customer Information Affidavit

D. Customer Information Order

Question 85

What is the primary risk of correspondence accounts?

> A. Recordkeeping because CDD rules do not apply to the Respondent Bank's clients.
>
> B. Money laundering because the final beneficiary is usually a druglord
>
> C. Money laundering because the final beneficiary is usually foreign
>
> D. Money laundering because for the Correspondence Bank, the funds might look like a single account.

Question 86

Who is the PEP with the most exposure?

> A. Winston Churchill, late former prime minister of British
>
> B. Skakira, Colombian singer
>
> C. JJ Abrans, Director of Star Wars: The Force Awkens
>
> D. François Hollande, President of France

Question 87

Which two are phases of Money Laundering?

    A. Layering and Structuring

    B. Placement and Integration

    C. Layering and Smurfing

    D. Structuring and Integration

Question 88

Which activities are associated with black market peso exchanges?

    A. Purchase of US goods in the US with illicit drug proceeds to be exported to Colombia.

    B. Purchase of Colombian drugs with Colombian Pesos in the US to be converted into US dollars for US bank deposit.

    C. Purchase of Colombian export products to be sold in the US with illicit drugs hidden in the shipments.

    D. Purchase of US student visas from Colombian exchange students to sneak into the US.

Question 89

Which of the following are methods of money laundering at a casino?

> A. Depositing legitimate earnings from gambling into a prepaid credit card and sending the credit card to help terrorist.
>
> B. Spending free reward points the casino has provided on the casino's hotel for lodging.
>
> C. Meeting with a dealer ahead of time to setup a strategy to fix the blackjack table.
>
> D. Depositing illicit funds and gambling winnings at the casino in Las Vegas and then taking the money out in Atlantic City.

Question 90

Which of the following are appropriate ways to reduce money laundering risk in correspondent banking?

> A. File a CTR for ever transaction performed through a correspondent banking account.
>
> B. File an SAR for every transaction performed through a correspondent banking account.
>
> C. Require identification information of those working at the bank receiving the correspondence services.
>
> D. Require identification information of those receiving the services at the account holding bank.

Question 91

Which scenarios require an SAR?

    A. New customer deposits $100,000 into the checking account and tries to withdraw all of it the next day.

    B. A customer deposits funds consistently at a bank branch closest to his office.

    C. A customer withdraws frequently from an area of the city with lots of restaurants.

    D. A customer deposits varying amounts just below the reporting threshold on a daily basis for a week.

Question 92

Which of the following should be included in an investigation log?

    A. Government order on a customer that garnishes is wages for failure to pay child support.

    B. Supporting documentation and materials for denying service to a client with a bad credit rating.

    C. Notes pertaining to activity that is unusual, but for which a STR has not been filed.

    D. Reference to a memorandum to the company's corporate management relating to budgetary and similar concerns.

Question 93

To which organization does a financial institution must submit CTRs?

      A. OFAC

      B. DOJ

      C. FBI

      D. FinCEN

Question 94

CTRs must be filed for currency activity (single and multiple transactions) below the $10,000 reporting requirement when the activity is greater than...

      A. $4,000.00

      B. $5,000.00

      C. $6,000.00

      D. $7,000.00

Question 95

CTRs must be filed for currency transactions involving multiple lower dollar transactions that over a period of time aggregate to a substantial sum of money when the dollar amount of the aggregate is...

>   A. Under $10,000

>   B. Over $10,000

>   C. Over $30,000

>   D. Undefined

Question 96

CTRs must be filed for currency transactions involving multiple lower dollar transactions that over a period of time aggregate to a substantial sum of money when the dollar amount of the individual transaction are...

>   A. Under $3,000

>   B. Over $3,000

>   C. Over $10,000

>   D. Undefined

Question 97

For fund transfers, banks must maintain records in amounts of...

     A. $30,000 and above

     B. $10,000 and above

     C. $7,000 and above

     D. $3,000 and above

Question 98

For monetary instruments, banks must maintain records in amounts of...

     A. $30,000 and above

     B. $10,000 and above

     C. $7,000 and above

     D. $3,000 and above

Question 99

Who is PEP with the most exposure?

    A. Kalpit Shah, Sr VP of compliance strategy at a regional bank

    B. Helen Zaltzman, Host of The Allusionist

    C. Ira Glass, Host of This American Life

    D. Malala Yousafzai, Nobel Peace Prize Winner

Question 100

Who is PEP with the most exposure?

    A. Misty Copeland, ballerina

    B. Michelle Quan, retired figure skater

    C. John Hodgman, comedian

    D. Park Geun Hye, President of Republic of Korea

Question 101

Who is PEP with the most exposure?

      A. Adrian Butcher, compliance officer at a regional bank

      B. Lee Changho, associate at an architectural firm

      C. Peter Sagal, host of Wait, Wait Don't Tell Me

      D. Tony Blair, former prime minister of Britain

Question 102

Who is PEP with the most exposure?

      A. Dao Nguyen, publisher at Buzzfeed

      B. Alexander Chee, author of The Queen of the Night

      C. Xue Jiang, designer at Misook

      D. Ivanka Trump, daughter of Donald Trump

Question 103

Which are criteria for assessing customer AML risk?

A. Use of other products and services at the institution.

B. Provides full identification information.

C. Relationships with employees at the institution.

D. Credit Rating.

Question 104

Which are criteria for assessing customer AML risk?

A. Regular automatic deposits from known employer

B. High checking account balance

C. High savings account balance

D. Several cash deposits made for several days, each at $7,000

Question 105

You are a compliance officer at a large bank. Kim Thuy is a customer with a business checking account who is involved in the import-export business. For a number of reasons, her account has been flagged, so, you review it. Though the account has been open for nine years, for the past eight months a number of SARs have been filed due to suspicious transactions. A regulatory enforcement agent has picked up the case and has contacted you. You ask the agent to advise you about what to do with the account. The agent does not advise. Which of the following should is the most appropriate decision?

A. Terminate all relationships with this this customer.

B. Terminate just this account but let the customer start a new account.

C. Contact the account owner again about the nature of suspicious transactions.

D. Ask the agent to advise again.

Question 106

You are a compliance officer at a regional bank that is trying find a better vendor for CDD/KYC analysis. Which of the following should be part of the criteria for acceptance of the vendor product?

A. The products ability to work with the existing systems in the bank.

B. The vendor's ability to train bank employees on the product.

C. The product's ability to perform CDD/KYC analysis to the bank's requirements.

D. The product's ability to match the color schemes of the bank's systems.

Question 107

You are a compliance officer at a regional bank. You read in the news that Jay Kristoff, an American, has been found to be fighting for ISIS in Syria. You should…

        A. Check to see if the Mets lost yet another game to the Yankees.

        B. Send out an all alert to the whole bank to see the bank has any associations with Kristoff..

        C. Check for accounts at your bank that could be under his name when you get into the office.

        D. Check for accounts at your bank that could be under his name when he is listed on FBI's Wanted List.

Question 108

You are a compliance officer at a global money exchanger. Your business charges no fees for exchanging currencies retail, but does add a premium to the rate of exchange. Each branch is given daily updates to the rate for that business day, but occasionally, the branch manger must manually enter the rates. Each branch is open during normal business hours customary to the area it serves. Which of the following should be of concern to you.

        A. Whether the manual rate changes are inputted correctly.

        B. Whether the cash till for each currency exchanged and the reported amounts match.

        C. Whether the manual rate changes are made when they are supposed to be made.

        D. Whether the branch uniforms are worn in compliance with the corporate dress code.

Question 109

You are a junior compliance officer at a large bank. You attend a AML conference and learn of a new requirement that will be implemented in six months. When you get back in the office, you should…

        A. Get back to work and assume the senior compliance officers already know about the new requirement.

        B. Check with the appropriate regulator to see if your bank could be given more time to meet the requirements.

        C. Check with the appropriate senior compliance officer to see whether the bank is prepared for the new requirement.

        D. Check with the appropriate senior compliance officer to see whether the bank is prepared to evade the new requirement.

Question 110

You read in the newspaper that Robert Palmer, a historian, has been involved in a financial crime. Your research shows that he is a long time customer of the bank. Your research also shows that there has been no suspicious activity in his accounts. What should you do next?

        A. Close the customer's accounts.

        B. Document the findings and appropriately file them for later reference.

        C. File an STR anyway because he is a known suspect and all of his transactions are now under scrutiny.

        D. Contact the agency investigator to offer the customer's account history.

Question 111

You are a compliance consultant hired to assess a broker-dealer's compliance program. Which of the following are you should be looking for?

A. Whether the compliance program is tested by someone independent from compliance.

B. Whether all employees, managers, and directors of the board are required to go through compliance training.

C. Whether there is a designated compliance officer.

D. Whether the compliance staff are adequately trained in the products and services of the business.

Question 112

Alain de Botton is a philosopher-writer and a client at your broker-dealer, where you are a compliance officer. He has opened an account with the goal of amounting retirement savings. Which of the following activities should you be concerned about in terms of AML?

A. The dividend returns from one fund is used to purchase government bonds within the account.

B. The funds have been invested in a automatically diversifying fund.

C. There are no investments made with the funds that were wire-transferred in.

D. There is a consistent transfer of funds into the account.

Question 113

Alexander Chee owns a corporation in Paris, which owns a corporation in Seoul, which owns a corporation in the US. The Paris corporation lends money to the Seoul corporation while the Seoul corporation lends money to the US corporation. When the US corporation pays back the loan to the Seoul corporation, the Seoul corporation pays back the loan to the Paris corporation. This scheme is known as a...

        A. Intra-corporate loan.

        B. Loan back.

        C. Intra-jurisdiction loan.

        D. Profit funnel.

Question 114

Jung Yun walks into a stockbroker's office and asks to open a trading account. She informs the broker that she has never done any investment trading before. Which of the following states would raise a red flag?

        A. She asks no questions about investment returns or risks.

        B. She decides to open an account.

        C. She does not ask about how much it would cost.

        D. Her business address and her home address are the same.

Question 115

Rainbow Rowell walks into a bank branch and asks to open a business checking account. Which of the following would raise a red flag?

        A. She wants to deposit $1 Million, which she has no explanation for its origins.

        B. Her business and home addresses are on the other side of the city.

        C. Her credit rating is good.

        D. She is reluctant to share information about the type of business she runs.

Question 116

Don DeLillo has a business checking account and a personal checking out at the same bank. He owns a muffin factory, so, he usually cuts pay checks weekly. He also cuts himself a check weekly and each quarter, he cuts himself an additional check so that his balance begins the quarter at $15,000. His factory primarily sells to department stores and high end retail stores. Which of the following would raise a red flag?

        A. He starts cutting an additional check in the middle of a quarter to a new employee.

        B. He makes a series of cash deposits, each under $5,000.

        C. Soon after a new employee starts getting paid, he receives additional deposits from sales.

        D. He makes a series of cash withdrawals, each under $5,000.

Question 117

You are a compliance officer. H. G. Wells is a banker that works with you in a bank branch. For the past several months, he has been complaining about how much high his mortgage payments are. Last week, he made a number of manual wire transfers from one customer to another customer. Their records show no relationship between the two. Which AML red flag would this activity raise?

        A. Assistance to a Black Market Peso Exchange.

        B. Facilitating a cuckoo smurf.

        C. Providing a front business.

        D. No red flag.

Question 118

Harper Lee is a a new customer at your investment firm. Which of the following would be an AML red flag?

        A. She is an American author.

        B. She wired $100,000 but has not any investments in the past 6 months.

        C. She completes all of the fields in the required onboarding application.

        D. She claims he made his money from selling bestselling novels.

Question 119

Jaap van Zweden is a new customer seeking life insurance products. Which of the following would an AML red flag?

A. He makes his wife his first beneficiary upon his death.

B. He makes full use of the free lookback period.

C. He takes a loss and ends the contract.

D. He reads the insurance contract carefully.

Question 120

You are a compliance officer. One of your bank's customers is a Seiji Ozawa, a luxury yacht builder in the Principality of Monaco. He has setup an account to receive payments from sales. The records show that he used to receive wire transfers for all of his sales across the United States, but he started receiving transfers from a correspondent bank account under his own name. Which of the following are AML red flags?

A. The account he setup to receive his sales proceeds had transfers out to his personal checking account.

B. The correspondent bank account in his own name suggests that he is making sales abroad but the payments origins are unknown.

C. The correspondent bank account in his own name suggests that he is moving his business abroad.

D. The account he setup to receive his sales proceeds never received real sales.

ANSWERS

1. _____

2. _____

3. _____

4. _____

5. _____

6. _____

7. _____

8. _____

9. _____

10. _____

11. _____

12. _____

13. _____

14. _____

15. _____

16. _____

17. _____

18. _____

19. _____

20. _____

21. _____

22. _____

23. _____

24. _____

25. _____

26. _____

27. _____

28. _____

29. _____

30. _____

31. _____

32. _____

33. _____

34. _____

35. _____

36. _____

37. _____

38. _____

39. _____

40. _____

41. _____

42. _____

43. _____

44. _____

45. _____

46. _____

47. _____

48. _____

49. _____

50. _____

51. _____

52. _____

53. _____

54. _____

55. _____

56. _____

57. _____

58. _____

59. _____

60. _____

61. _____

62. _____

63. _____

64. _____

65. _____

66. _____

67. _____

68. _____

69. _____

70. _____

71. _____

72. _____

73. _____

74. _____

75. _____

76. _____

77. _____

78. _____

79. _____

80. _____

81. _____

82. _____

83. _____

84. _____

85. _____

86. _____

87. _____

88. _____

89. _____

90. _____

91. _____

92. _____

93. _____

94. _____

95. _____

96. _____

97. _____

98. _____

99. _____

100. _____

101. _____

102. _____

103. _____

104. _____

105. _____

106. _____

107. _____

108. _____

109. _____

110. _____

111. _____

112. _____

113. _____

114. _____

115. _____

116. _____

117. _____

118. _____

119. _____

120. _____

ANSWERS

1. _____A_____

2. _____B_____

3. _____D_____

4. _____B_____

5. _____D_____

6. _____A,B,C,D_____

7. _____A_____

8. _____A_____

9. _____B,C,D_____

10. _____C_____

11. _____B_____

12. _____B_____

13. _____A,B,C_____

14. _____A_____

15. _____A_____

16. _____B_____

17. _____B_____

18. _____A_____

19. _____A_____

20. _____A,B,C_____

21. _____D_____

22. _____A_____

23. _____A_____

24. _____B_____

25. _____D_____

26. _____A_____

27. _____A,B,C,D_____

28. _____A_____

29. _____A,D_____

30. _____A,B,C,D_____

31. _____A,B,C,D_____

32. _____D_____

33. _____A_____

34. _____A_____

35. _____D_____

36. _____D_____

37. _____D_____

38. _____D_____

39. _____D_____

40. ___D___

41. ___D___

42. ___B,C___

43. ___D___

44. ___D___

45. ___D___

46. ___D___

47. ___D___

48. ___D___

49. ___D___

50. ___D___

51. ___D___

52. ___D___

53. ___D___

54. ___D___

55. ___D___

56. ___D___

57. ___D___

58. ___D___

59. ___D___

60. ___D___

61. _____ D _____

62. _____ D _____

63. _____ D _____

64. _____ D _____

65. _____ D _____

66. _____ D _____

67. _____ D _____

68. _____ D _____

69. _____ D _____

70. _____ D _____

71. _____ D _____

72. _____ D _____

73. _____ D _____

74. _____ D _____

75. _____ A,B,C,D _____

76. _____ D _____

77. _____ D _____

78. _____ D _____

79. _____ D _____

80. _____ D _____

81. _____ A,B,C,D _____

82. _____D_____

83. _____D_____

84. _____D_____

85. _____D_____

86. _____D_____

87. _____B_____

88. _____A_____

89. _____D_____

90. _____D_____

91. _____A,D_____

92. _____C_____

93. _____D_____

94. _____D_____

95. _____D_____

96. _____D_____

97. _____D_____

98. _____D_____

99. _____D_____

100. _____D_____

101. _____D_____

102. _____D_____

103. _____A,B,C,D_____

104. _____D_____

105. _____A_____

106. _____A,B,C_____

107. _____C_____

108. _____A,B,C_____

109. _____C_____

110. _____B_____

111. _____A,B,C,D_____

112. _____C_____

113. _____B_____

114. _____A,C,D_____

115. _____A,B,D_____

116. _____B,D_____

117. _____B_____

118. _____B_____

119. _____B,C_____

120. _____B_____

CAMS Examination Practice Test One

Version Two

Question 1

FBI provides a bank with a warrant requesting account information on the bank's customer, who is a known terrorist suspect. The bank should...

      A. Provide the requested information after sending a notification to the customer.

      B. Not provide the requested information until the customer has provided approval to the bank.

      C. Provide the requested information.

      D. Not provide the requested information.

Question 2

Which of the following should a national legislature consider when criminalizing money laundering in line with FATF 19 Recommendations?

      A. Do no limit the number of specific predicate offenses for money laundering.

      B. Criminalize conspiracy or association to engage in money laundering.

      C. Indicate whether it is relevant that a predicate offense may have been committed outside the local jurisdiction.

      D. Require money laundering offenses to be proven with evidence that show that the offender had actual knowledge of a criminal connection to the funds.

Question 3

Which of the following are money laundering risks associated with Broker-Dealers?

A. Ease of converting currencies and financial products.

B. Brokerage firms provide anonymity from the market by being named nominee/trustee of client funds.

C. Commission-driven environment pressures broker-dealers to cut corners.

D. Speed of transactions.

Question 4

What is International Money Laundering Information Network (IMoLIN)?

A. A division of Financial Crimes Enforcement Network (FinCEN).

B. An Internet-based network assisting governments, organizations and individuals in the fight against money laundering.

C. A network of best money launders where they can share best practices.

D. A network of corporate governance, risk, and compliance professionals around the world.

Question 5

CDD is the abbreviation for...

      A. Core Data Dumps

      B. Corporate Data Definitions

      C. Customer Due Diligence

      D. Duties

Question 6

What is International Narcotics Control Strategy Report?

      A. Annual report on the state of drug trafficking and money laundering issued by the United Nations.

      B. Annual report on the efforts of the CDC to treat patients addicted to various illicit drugs.

      C. Annual report on the state of drug trafficking and money laundering issued by the US Department of State.

      D. Biannual report on the state of drug trafficking and money laundering issued by the Office of the Chancellor of the Exchequer.

Question 7

What is an offshore bank?

> A. A alternative remitter that serves the underbanked in developing economies.

> B. A bank that is not licensed to provide banking services in foreign currencies.

> C. A bank that insures insurance companies for casualty insurance plans.

> D. A bank that is not licensed to provide banking services in domestic currency.

Question 8

What is the Wolfsberg Group?

> A. Group of 7 Finance Ministers that have agreed on a set of AML guidelines.

> B. Group of 11 large banks that have agreed on a set of AML guidelines.

> C. Group of 20 central bank governors that have agreed on a set of AML guidelines.

> D. Group of 24 developing countries that have agreed on a set of AML guidelines.

Question 9

Which of the following are appropriate ways to reduce money laundering risk in correspondent banking?

> A. File a CTR for ever transaction performed through a correspondent banking account.
>
> B. File an SAR for every transaction performed through a correspondent banking account.
>
> C. Require identification information of those working at the bank receiving the correspondence services.
>
> D. Require identification information of those receiving the services at the account holding bank.

Question 10

Who is PEP with the most exposure?

> A. Park Geun Hye, President of Republic of Korea
>
> B. Misty Copeland, ballerina
>
> C. Michelle Quan, retired figure skater
>
> D. John Hodgman, comedian

Question 11

You read in the newspaper that Robert Palmer, a historian, has been involved in a financial crime. Your research shows that he is a long time customer of the bank. Your research also shows that there has been no suspicious activity in his accounts. What should you do next?

A. Close the customer's accounts.

B. Document the findings and appropriately file them for later reference.

C. File an STR anyway because he is a known suspect and all of his transactions are now under scrutiny.

D. Contact the agency investigator to offer the customer's account history.

Question 12

You are a compliance officer. One of your bank's customers is a Seiji Ozawa, a luxury yacht builder in the Principality of Monaco. He has setup an account to receive payments from sales. The records show that he used to receive wire transfers for all of his sales across the United States, but he started receiving transfers from a correspondent bank account under his own name. Which of the following are AML red flags?

A. The account he setup to receive his sales proceeds had transfers out to his personal checking account.

B. The correspondent bank account in his own name suggests that he is making sales abroad but the payments origins are unknown.

C. The correspondent bank account in his own name suggests that he is moving his business abroad.

D. The account he setup to receive his sales proceeds never received real sales.

Question 13

Which of the following cannot be a method of money laundering?

A. Cuckoo smurfing

B. Black Market Peso Exchange

C. Payable Through Accounts

D. Purchasing Structured Financial Products

Question 14

When a financial institution is responding to a formal criminal investigation by a law enforcement agency, what is the primary purpose of requiring information going through a central point within the institution?

A. To be able to ensure that nothing damaging to the financial institution gets released.

B. To ensure that responses are timely and thorough, and that privileged material is not inadvertently handed over.

C. To ensure that the employees of the institution do not divulge information that would breach the privacy rights of customers.

D. To ensure that there is one person who can adequately and thoroughly apprise the Board of Directors of the progress of the investigation.

Question 15

The FATF 40 Recommendations say that countries should…

A. Not allow bearer shares and legal persons that are able to issue bearer shares.

B. Gather statistics on STRs; prosecutions and convictions; and provide mutual legal assistance, but not necessarily on other international requests for cooperation.

C. Consider the feasibility of a system where banks and other financial institutions and intermediaries would report currency transactions without indicating a minimum fixed amount.

D. Not approve the establishment or accept the continued operation of shell banks.

Question 16

What is the risk associated with real estate industry?

A. Broker's escrow accounts normally have large and diverse transactions taking place, making it ideal for laundering.

B. Construction expenses are easily manipulated for purposes of laundering, especially when the launderer is the acting as contractor.

C. High percentage of money laundering cases involves real estate.

D. Rural properties are ideal for growing and storing drugs.

Question 17

What is Bank Secrecy Act?

      A. An addendum to the 1930 Advisers Act

      B. 1970 US legislation that requires reporting and recordkeeping at financial institutions.

      C. 1972 US legislation that requires banks to maintain absolute secrecy about the identity of their clients.

      D. A major part of the USA PATRIOT Act of 2001.

Question 18

What is a Downstream Correspondent Clearer?

      A. A clearing house for checks that were endorsed by the recipient to pay a secondary recipient.

      B. A clearing house within the US Postal Service that delivers certified government checks.

      C. A correspondence banking client that provides banking services to its own clients through the correspondence account.

      D. A correspondence bank that provides banking services to correspondence banking client.

Question 19

Placement

    A. First phase of money laundering with the goal of entering the legitimate financial system

    B. Second phase of money laundering with the goal of obfuscating the origin of the placed funds.

    C. Third phase of money laundering with the goal of using the laundered funds for a legitimate purpose.

    D. Fourth phase of money laundering with the goal of using legitimate funds for illegitimate purposes.

Question 20

What is a payable through account?

    A. A bank account for a retail merchant just for paying business expenses.

    B. A bank account opened by another bank on behalf of client in order for that client to receive banking services.

    C. A bank account opened by another bank on behalf of client in order evade disclosure rules.

    D. A bank account opened by a non-bank client who seek to provide unlicensed banking services.

Question 21

What are the minimum requirements for an effective AML program?

A. Designated AML compliance officer

B. Independent review to test the program

C. On-going employee training

D. Written internal policies, procedures and controls

Question 22

Which scenarios require an SAR?

A. New customer deposits $100,000 into the checking account and tries to withdraw all of it the next day.

B. A customer deposits funds consistently at a bank branch closest to his office.

C. A customer withdraws frequently from an area of the city with lots of restaurants.

D. A customer deposits varying amounts just below the reporting threshold on a daily basis for a week.

Question 23

Who is PEP with the most exposure?

    A. Lee Changho, associate at an architectural firm

    B. Tony Blair, former prime minister of Britain

    C. Adrian Butcher, compliance officer at a regional bank

    D. Peter Sagal, host of Wait, Wait Don't Tell Me

Question 24

You are a compliance consultant hired to assess a broker-dealer's compliance program. Which of the following are you should be looking for?

    A. Whether the compliance program is tested by someone independent from compliance.

    B. Whether all employees, managers, and directors of the board are required to go through compliance training.

    C. Whether there is a designated compliance officer.

    D. Whether the compliance staff are adequately trained in the products and services of the business.

Question 25

Which of the following is an indication of possible money laundering?

> A. An automobile insurance plan bought through an insurance agent.
>
> B. Redemption of bond at significant discount.
>
> C. Purchasing a mutual fund and individual stocks for a single account with a broker-dealer.
>
> D. A financial adviser selling a Credit Derivative Swap to an ambitious young professional opening an IRA.

Question 26

When should a financial institution consider retaining an experienced outside counsel to assist it?

> A. Whenever the institution receives a subpoena from any law enforcement agency.
>
> B. When the institution itself appears to be the target of a criminal investigation.
>
> C. When law enforcement appears to be focused on the accounts of a very good and long-standing customer of the institution.
>
> D. When the banking agencies criticize the adequacy of the institution's AML monitoring procedures.

Question 27

According to the FATF 40 Recommendations, "designated non-financial businesses and professionals" include...

A. Casinos, real estate agents and dealers in precious stones.

B. Money service businesses, a, gatekeepers, and issuers of electronic money.

C. Dealers in precious metals, lawyers, commodity futures traders.

D. Life insurance companies, real estate agents and notaries.

Question 28

What is the risk associated with prepaid credit/debit cards?

A. Like cash, it can be anonymous.

B. Like checks, it has a definite associated identification.

C. Like loans, it has an application process.

D. Like travelers checks, it requires signature.

Question 29

What is Bank Secrecy Act? Matthew Salesses is a new customer seeking life insurance products. Which of the following would an AML red flag?

      A. He makes full use of the free lookback period.

      B. He makes his wife his first beneficiary upon his death.

      C. He reads the insurance contract carefully.

      D. He takes a loss and ends the contract.

Question 30

EFT is an abbreviation for...

      A. Electronic Financial Transaction

      B. Electronic Fraud Transverse

      C. Electronic Funds Transfer

      D. Exchange Funded Transfer

Question 31

Layering

    A. First phase of money laundering with the goal of entering the legitimate financial system

    B. Second phase of money laundering with the goal of obfuscating the origin of the placed funds.

    C. Third phase of money laundering with the goal of using the laundered funds for a legitimate purpose.

    D. Fourth phase of money laundering with the goal of using legitimate funds for illegitimate purposes.

Question 32

What is a predicate crime?

    A. Crimes are gambling with investor money in casinos rather than in the strategy laid out in the prospectus.

    B. Crimes underlying legitimate business activity with illicit proceeds.

    C. Crimes underlying money laundering or terrorist finance activity.

    D. Money laundering or terrorist finance activity are predicate crimes.

Question 33

What is the primary benefit advertised for Asset Protection Trusts (APTs)?

    A. Domestic trustees may not have to comply with US courts.

    B. EU trustees may not have to comply with US courts.

    C. Foreign trustees may not have to comply with US courts.

    D. US trustees may not have to comply with EU courts.

Question 34

Which of the following should be included in an investigation log?

    A. Government order on a customer that garnishes wages for failure to pay child support.

    B. Notes pertaining to activity that is unusual, but for which a STR has not been filed.

    C. Reference to a memorandum to the company's corporate management relating to budgetary and similar concerns.

    D. Supporting documentation and materials for denying service to a client with a bad credit rating.

Question 35

Who is PEP with the most exposure?

A. Alexander Chee, author of The Queen of the Night

B. Dao Nguyen, publisher at Buzzfeed

C. Ivanka Trump, daughter of Donald Trump

D. Xue Jiang, designer at Misook

Question 36

Alain de Botton is a philosopher-writer and a client at your broker-dealer, where you are a compliance officer. He has opened an account with the goal of amounting retirement savings. Which of the following activities should you be concerned about in terms of AML?

A. The dividend returns from one fund is used to purchase government bonds within the account.

B. The funds have been invested in a automatically diversifying fund.

C. There are no investments made with the funds that were wire-transferred in.

D. There is a consistent transfer of funds into the account.

Question 37

A method of laundering money through international trade is by...

      A. Both, over- and under-invoicing of goods

      B. Do not invoice for goods

      C. Only over-invoicing of goods

      D. Only under-invoicing of goods

Question 38

What are practical tips in interviewing employees with regard to an unusual or suspicious transaction that they have witnessed?

      A. Interview the employees as soon after the occurrence as possible in order to ensure that their memories are fresh.

      B. Put the employees at ease during the interview and start with relatively easy, non-controversial, questions before getting into more sensitive matters.

      C. Use open-ended questions for the employees in order to ensure that the questions do not dictate what the expected answer is.

      D. Control the interview as much as possible in order to attempt to resolve the matter quickly and uncover the wrongdoer.

Question 39

FATF has consistently noted the use of casinos in money laundering schemes in its annual typologies reports. One laundering technique involving casinos is...

        A. Asking for winner's checks to be made out in the name of third persons or without a payee.

        B. Abusing casinos by circumventing its gatekeepers.

        C. Prepaying a casino token or chip by using funds that are already in the casino system, creating a debit balance.

        D. Extensive gambling via multiple games through the casino.

Question 40

Which group is the most important to get buy-in when developing an AML Program?

        A. Internal Audit

        B. IT

        C. Legal

        D. Senior Management

Question 41

What is a bare trust?

      A. A special trust in Sharia Law that allows lending of money to those within the family.

      B. A trust account that has little or no funds.

      C. A trust account where the ultimate beneficial owner must reveal all assets within to the government.

      D. A trust where the trustee has only one duty, which is to convey the trust assets to the named beneficiary at the appropriate time.

Question 42

What is an extradition?

      A. The act of transferring funds in the tradition of the local jurisdiction.

      B. The act of extracting identification of potential financing of terrorism.

      C. A method of corporate espionage where the spy is embedded for years inside of a bank to discover security weaknesses.

      D. Often requiring a treaty for it to take place, the act of surrendering a person by one country to another country.

Question 43

Integration

A. First phase of money laundering with the goal of entering the legitimate financial system

B. Second phase of money laundering with the goal of obfuscating the origin of the placed funds.

C. Third phase of money laundering with the goal of using the laundered funds for a legitimate purpose.

D. Fourth phase of money laundering with the goal of using legitimate funds for illegitimate purposes.

Question 44

What is the Report on the Observance of Standards and Codes (ROSC)?

A. Report that summarizes the efforts of the World Bank and IMF to implementing international AML and anti-graft standards.

B. Report that summarizes the efforts of the World Bank and IMF to implementing international accounting and auditing standards.

C. Report that summarizes the efforts of the OECD and ADB to implementing international AML and anti-graft standards.

D. Report that summarizes the efforts of the OECD and ADB to implementing international accounting and auditing standards.

Question 45

At a casino, STRs must be filed for transactions greater than...

      A. $3,000

      B. $7,000

      C. $10,000

      D. $25,000

Question 46

To which organization does a financial institution must submit CTRs?

      A. DOJ

      B. FBI

      C. FinCEN

      D. OFAC

Question 47

Which are criteria for assessing customer AML risk?

    A. Credit Rating.

    B. Provides full identification information.

    C. Relationships with employees at the institution.

    D. Use of other products and services at the institution.

Question 48

Misook Kim owns a corporation in Paris, which owns a corporation in Seoul, which owns a corporation in the US. The Paris corporation lends money to the Seoul corporation while the Seoul corporation lends money to the US corporation. When the US corporation pays back the loan to the Seoul corporation, the Seoul corporation pays back the loan to the Paris corporation. This scheme is known as a...

    A. Intra-corporate loan.

    B. Intra-jurisdiction loan.

    C. Loan back.

    D. Profit funnel.

Question 49

What is considered a beneficial owner of an account?

Person or Entity that...

> A. Is the person or entity on legal documents.
>
> B. Is ultimately entitled to the funds in the account.
>
> C. Will inherit the funds in the account at the death of the account holder.
>
> D. Is representing a client who has the claim to the funds.

Question 50

When a bank receives a subpoena, the bank should first...

> A. Begin a social media campaign to mitigate any negative consequences.
>
> B. Immediately notify the Board of Directors.
>
> C. Start its own investigation internally.
>
> D. Sue the account holder that caused the subpoena in the amount of the total cost it took to response properly to the subpoena.

Question 51

In what year did the EU adopt the *First Directive on Prevention of the Use of the Financial System for the Purpose of Money Laundering*

      A. 1988

      B. 1991

      C. 2001

      D. 2005

Question 52

What would be the most effective way to keep senior management updated on the efficacy of the AML Program?

      A. Provide a report with metrics of the key elements of the program for a given period, compare it to a relevant period and against a stated measurable goal.

      B. Provide a report that shows how much money was spent on the AML Program.

      C. Provide a report of the number of SARs and STRs that have been filed.

      D. Provide a report describing a representative experience of an employee's involvement in the compliance program.

Question 53

What is a bearer share certificate?

    A. A corporate debt certificate that gives the right to convert it to equity shares at a certain share price.

    B. A corporate equity share certificate of a bank holding company.

    C. A corporate equity certificate that a shareholder can print from home or office.

    D. A corporate equity share certificate with its ownership given to the person holding it.

Question 54

What is the mission of FATF?

    A. To administer and enforce economic and trade sanctions based on US foreign policy and national security goals.

    B. To provide loans to developing countries for capital program.

    C. To review and grant special financing for defendants at the International Criminal Court in the Haag.

    D. To set standards and promote effective implementation of legal, regulatory and operational measures for combating money laundering and terrorist financing.

Question 55

What is the loan back method?

    A. A way to launder money by borrowing money and then paying back the money with the illicit funds.

    B. A way to launder money by over-paying taxes and then to receive a refund later to receive a government check.

    C. A way to provide mortgage loans to those who defaulted for the same house and same terms as the previous loan.

    D. A way to swap an existing loan with the bank for a new loan in order for the bank to record lower risk rating to cheat the Federal Reserve requirements.

Question 56

What is retrospective due diligence?

    A. Due diligence of closed accounts.

    B. Due diligence of the due diligence practices of the bank.

    C. Due diligence performed on existing customers.

    D. Due diligence of returning new customers.

Question 57

What is a document that allows a financial institution to release customer information to an appropriate government investigator?

      A. Customer Information Affidavit

      B. Customer Information Form

      C. Customer Information Order

      D. Customer Information Request

Question 58

CTRs must be filed for currency activity (single and multiple transactions) below the $10,000 reporting requirement when the activity is greater than...

      A. $3,000.00

      B. $5,000.00

      C. $7,000.00

      D. $15,000.00

Question 59

Which are criteria for assessing customer AML risk?

    A. High checking account balance

    B. High savings account balance

    C. Regular automatic deposits from known employer

    D. Several cash deposits made for several days, each at $7,000

Question 60

Jung Yun walks into a stockbroker's office and asks to open a trading account. She informs the broker that she has never done any investment trading before. Which of the following states would raise a red flag?

    A. She asks no questions about investment returns or risks.

    B. She decides to open an account.

    C. She does not ask about how much it would cost.

    D. Her business address and her home address are the same.

Question 61

What activity is it when a depositor makes multiple deposits to evade the bank's reporting threshold?

      A. Dividing

      B. Integrating

      C. Layering

      D. Structuring

Question 62

When a new customer immediately transfers the initial deposits to a foreign bank, the compliance officer should first...

      A. File a preliminary STR or SAR.

      B. Contact the financial regulator of that jurisdiction.

      C. Start an investigation.

      D. Notify the Board of Directors.

Question 63

In what year did the EU adopt the *Third Directive on Prevention of the Use of the Financial System for the Purpose of Money Laundering*

     A. 1988

     B. 1991

     C. 2001

     D. 2005

Question 64

In order to deter money laundering...

     A. Banks should have an internal secret police.

     B. Banks should encourage employees to snoop on each other.

     C. Banks should advertise ways to avert tax authorities.

     D. Banks should make a telephone hotline available to report activities anonymously.

Question 65

What is a bureau de change?

      A. Change Management Office of the Federal Government.

      B. French exchange for commodities and currencies.

      C. A retail currency exchanger.

      D. A special piece of furniture for metal coins.

Question 66

FIU is an abbreviation for...

      A. Federation of Insurance Underwriters

      B. Federalist Interpretation Union

      C. Financial Intelligence Unit

      D. Financial Intelligence United

Question 67

What is a lockbox?

A. A box that can be used to store sensitive items in a bank vault.

B. A box that holds the server location of all of the bank's client accounts.

C. A service offered by banks where the bank will pay the invoices and withdrawal funds on behalf of the client.

D. A service offered by banks where the bank will receive payments in a post office box and makes the deposits on behalf of the client.

Question 68

What is an example of a Self Regulatory Organization?

A. American Bar Association

B. American Institute of Certified Public Accountants

C. FINRA

D. New York Stock Exchange

Question 69

What is the primary risk of correspondence accounts?

       A. Money laundering because the final beneficiary is usually a druglord

       B. Money laundering because the final beneficiary is usually foreign

       C. Money laundering because for the Correspondence Bank, the funds might look like a single account.

       D. Recordkeeping because CDD rules do not apply to the Respondent Bank's clients.

Question 70

CTRs must be filed for currency transactions involving multiple lower dollar transactions that over a period of time aggregate to a substantial sum of money when the dollar amount of the aggregate is...

       A. Under $10,000

       B. Over $10,000

       C. Over $30,000

       D. Undefined

Question 71

You are a compliance officer at a large bank. Kim Thuy is a customer with a business checking account who is involved in the import-export business. For a number of reasons, her account has been flagged, so, you review it. Though the account has been open for nine years, for the past eight months a number of SARs have been filed due to suspicious transactions. A regulatory enforcement agent has picked up the case and has contacted you. You ask the agent to advise you about what to do with the account. The agent does not advise. Which of the following should is the most appropriate decision?

A. Ask the agent to advise again.

B. Contact the account owner again about the nature of suspicious transactions.

C. Terminate all relationships with this this customer.

D. Terminate just this account but let the customer start a new account.

Question 72

Rainbow Rowell walks into a bank branch and asks to open a business checking account. Which of the following would raise a red flag?

A. Her business and home addresses are on the other side of the city.

B. Her credit rating is good.

C. She is reluctant to share information about the type of business she runs.

D. She wants to deposit $1 Million, which she has no explanation for its origins.

Question 73

What are the goals of AML Programs?

    A. Prevent and detect money laundering and terrorist financing.

    B. Provide training to employees about the detection, policies, and procedures pertaining to AML.

    C. Report suspicious activities to FinCEN or other proper authorities of a given jurisdiction.

    D. Satisfy regulatory requirements.

Question 74

You are a compliance officer. One of your bank's customers is a Paavo Jarvi, a jeweler in New York. He has setup an account to receive payments from sales. The records show that he used to receive wire transfers for all of his sales across the Unite States, but he started receiving transfers from a correspondent bank account under his own name. Which of the following are AML red flag?

    A. The account he setup to receive his sales proceeds had transfers out to his personal checking account.

    B. The account he setup to receive his sales proceeds never received real sales.

    C. The correspondent bank account in his own name suggest that he is making sales abroad but the payments origins are unknown.

    D. The correspondent bank account in his own name suggests that he is moving his business abroad.

Question 75

How many recommendations are there in the EU *Third Directive on the Prevention of the Use of the Financial System for the Purpose of Money Laundering and Terrorist Financing*

      A. 40

      B. 28

      C. 16

      D. 13

Question 76

A money laundering risk associated with charities and non-profit organizations is...

      A. That these entities might have been created to evade taxes.

      B. That these entities are sometimes involved with the poor and the sick.

      C. That some of these entities run major sports leagues.

      D. That these entities might have been created specifically to launder money.

Question 77

What is a Bust-Out?

A. A scheme to bankrupt a company in order to reorganize and agree with lenders to bust-out previous loans.

B. A scheme to infiltrate a money laundering network by providing them with the sales of fake drugs.

C. A scheme to provide my to a company that needs funds for an expansion project but to write in covenants that make the financing of the expansion impossible.

D. A scheme to run and hide with loan proceeds that are greater than the value of the borrower company or property, leaving lender to take a loss at bankruptcy.

Question 78

What is a front company?

A. A company that receives the revenues for tax purposes even though the products are sold by another company, both owned wholly by a third company.

B. A company setup in a foreign jurisdiction with no corporate address or named executives or board members.

C. A legitimate business used as a vehicle for laundering money.

D. A limited liability company that is owned by a publicly traded corporation.

Question 79

What is a Mock Trial on Money Laundering?

A. A joint program of the UNODC and CICAD that teaches governments how to investigate and prosecute crimes.

B. A law school program sanctioned by the ABA and overseen by the DOJ to teach law students for a career in prosecution of financial crimes.

C. A program that helps FBI and DEA agents practice testifying in court on financial crimes prosecution.

D. A practice by the ICC to let each side practice their arguments against each other in order to refine application of laws.

Question 80

What is Structuring?

A. The practice of executing financial transactions in a specific pattern calculated to avoid reporting rules.

B. The practice of executing financial transactions in a specific pattern calculated to trigger reporting rules.

C. The practice of investing legitimate funds in the Black Market Peso Exchange to launder returns.

D. The practice of investing illicit funds in the capital markets to launder returns.

Question 81

Who is the PEP with the most exposure?

     A. François Hollande, President of France

     B. JJ Abrans, Director of Star Wars: The Force Awkens

     C. Skakira, Colombian singer

     D. Winston Churchill, late former prime minister of British

Question 82

CTRs must be filed for currency transactions involving multiple lower dollar transactions that over a period of time aggregate to a substantial sum of money when the dollar amount of the individual transaction are...

     A. Under $3,000

     B. Over $3,000

     C. Over $10,000

     D. Undefined

Question 83

You are a compliance officer at a regional bank that is trying find a better vendor for CDD/KYC analysis. Which of the following should be part of the criteria for acceptance of the vendor product?

A. The products ability to work with the existing systems in the bank.

B. The vendor's ability to train bank employees on the product.

C. The product's ability to perform CDD/KYC analysis to the bank's requirements.

D. The product's ability to match the color schemes of the bank's systems.

Question 84

Don DeLillo has a business checking account and a personal checking out at the same bank. He owns a muffin factory, so, he usually cuts pay checks weekly. He also cuts himself a check weekly and each quarter, he cuts himself an additional check so that his balance begins the quarter at $15,000. His factory primarily sells to department stores and high end retail stores. Which of the following would raise a red flag?

A. He makes a series of cash deposits, each under $5,000.

B. He makes a series of cash withdrawals, each under $5,000.

C. Soon after a new employee starts getting paid, he receives additional deposits from sales.

D. He starts cutting an additional check in the middle of a quarter to a new employee.

Question 85

How should the responsibility to comply be required?

        A. Make compliance a condition of employment.

        B. Make compliance an option that is rewarded with bonuses.

        C. Make employees swear an oath to compliance.

        D. Make internal audit check for efficacy of the internal controls.

Question 86

How should a compliance officer initially respond to a law enforcement inquiry?

        A. Cooperate fully as much as the laws allow.

        B. Cooperate after the law enforcement as agreed to a nondisclosure agreement.

        C. Refer law enforcement to outside counsel.

        D. Resist cooperation so that there is documented evidence that the bank tried to protect its customers and employees.

Question 87

EU *Third Directive on the Prevention of the Use of the Financial System for the Purpose of Money Laundering and Terrorist Financing* applies to...

A. Auditors

B. Bankers

C. Insurance brokers

D. Tax advisers

Question 88

What are the similarities between money laundering and terrorist financing?

A. Both activities could be a result of illicit activities.

B. Both activities are originate in Latin America.

C. Both activities are originate in the Middle East.

D. Both activities are a result of religious association.

Question 89

What is a Commission Rogatoire?

      A. A document permitting foreign subjects to perform investigations at French banks.

      B. A formal request to the French National Government to perform an investigation at a local bank.

      C. A formal request from one government to another government for legal or judicial assistance.

      D. An order by one government to another to provide legal or judicial assistance.

Question 90

What is a harmful or preferential tax regime?

      A. A country with very high taxes that makes business transactions expensive.

      B. A country with low or no tax rate in order to attract business.

      C. A military controlled state that is enforcing a kleptocracy.

      D. A US state with low or no tax rate in order to attract business.

Question 91

MSB is an abbreviation for...

      A. Money Sanctions Bank

      B. Money and Securities Business

      C. Money Services Business

      D. Mortgage Service Business

Question 92

SAR is an abbreviation for...

      A. Securitized Asset Report

      B. Suspended Activity Report

      C. Suspicious Activity Report

      D. Suspicious Adverse Report

Question 93

Which two are phases of Money Laundering?

A. Layering and Structuring

B. Placement and Integration

C. Layering and Smurfing

D. Structuring and Integration

Question 94

For fund transfers, banks must maintain records in amounts of...

A. $30,000 and above

B. $10,000 and above

C. $7,000 and above

D. $3,000 and above

Question 95

You are a compliance officer at a regional bank. You read in the news that Jay Kristoff, an American, has been found to be fighting for ISIS in Syria. You should...

    A. Check to see if the Mets lost yet another game to the Yankees.

    B. Send out an all alert to the whole bank to see the bank has any associations with Kristoff..

    C. Check for accounts at your bank that could be under his name when you get into the office.

    D. Check for accounts at your bank that could be under his name when he is listed on FBI's Wanted List.

Question 96

You are a compliance officer. H. G. Wells is a banker that works with you in a bank branch. For the past several months, he has been complaining about how much high his mortgage payments are. Last week, he made a number of manual wire transfers from one customer to another customer. Their records show no relationship between the two. Which AML red flag would this activity raise?

    A. Assistance to a Black Market Peso Exchange.

    B. Facilitating a cuckoo smurf.

    C. Providing a front business.

    D. No red flag.

Question 97

What should the compliance officer do after an appropriate regulatory investigator requests to interview the bank's employees?

A. Seek the bank's counsel's advice regarding the necessity of a subpoena or a warrant.

B. Ignore the request until a warrant or subpoena is presented.

C. Call the employee's manager to require the employee to be interviewed.

D. Seek the bank's counsel's advice regarding how to reject the request.

Question 98

EU *Third Directive on the Prevention of the Use of the Financial System for the Purpose of Money Laundering and Terrorist Financing* applies to which of the following firms?

A. Auditors, estate agents based in the EU.

B. US Financial institutions covered by the USA PATRIOT Act.

C. Shell firms inside and outside the EU.

D. EU based high value good dealers who deal in cash of 10,000 Euro or more.

Question 99

Which institution released the BSA/AML Examination Manual?

    A. FFIEC

    B. OCC

    C. FinCEN

    D. OFAC

Question 100

What is an Alternative Remittance System (ARS)?

    A. A payment system at the Bank of International Settlements for government transactions.

    B. A payment systems only for global corporations.

    C. A software that allows for wire transfers without the use of banks.

    D. A system of financial services provided by non-financial services firms, often in developing economies.

Question 101

What is cuckoo smurfing?

    A. An alternative remittance scheme that hides the transaction in an legitimate transaction of unrelated party, usually facilitated by a financial professional.

    B. A method of corporate espionage where the spy is embedded for years inside of a bank to discover security weaknesses.

    C. A method of hiding insider trading information (originally done inside photoshopped drawings of the Smurfs).

    D. A scheme of paying an investor with the funds received by a newer investor and calling it an investment return.

Question 102

What is a hawala?

    A. A system of merchants that provide fund transfers by using their ordinary trading business across borders.

    B. A system of merchants that provide short-term financing for local businesses without the use of a letter of credit.

    C. A system of merchant banks that provide fund transfers by using their ordinary trading business across borders.

    D. A traditional Indian method of accounting that used tea leaves and sacks of saffron to keep a record of inventory being warehoused by a common warehouse.

Question 103

MLAT is an abbreviation for...

    A. Mutual Legal Action Treaty

    B. Mutual Legal Assistance Tax

    C. Mutual Legal Assistance Treaty

    D. Mutual Legislative Action Treaty

Question 104

What is a typology?

    A. The methods of financing terrorism.

    B. The methods of financing front businesses.

    C. The methods of transporting narcotics.

    D. The methods of money laundering.

Question 105

Which activities are associated with black market peso exchanges?

> A. Purchase of US goods in the US with illicit drug proceeds to be exported to Colombia.
>
> B. Purchase of Colombian drugs with Colombian Pesos in the US to be converted into US dollars for US bank deposit.
>
> C. Purchase of Colombian export products to be sold in the US with illicit drugs hidden in the shipments.
>
> D. Purchase of US student visas from Colombian exchange students to sneak into the US.

Question 106

For monetary instruments, banks must maintain records in amounts of...

> A. $30,000 and above
>
> B. $10,000 and above
>
> C. $7,000 and above
>
> D. $3,000 and above

Question 107

You are a compliance officer at a global money exchanger. Your business charges no fees for exchanging currencies retail, but does add a premium to the rate of exchange. Each branch is given daily updates to the rate for that business day, but occasionally, the branch manger must manually enter the rates. Each branch is open during normal business hours customary to the area it serves. Which of the following should be of concern to you.

    A. Whether the manual rate changes are inputted correctly.

    B. Whether the cash till for each currency exchanged and the reported amounts match.

    C. Whether the manual rate changes are made when they are supposed to be made.

    D. Whether the branch uniforms are worn in compliance with the corporate dress code.

Question 108

Harper Lee is a new customer at your investment firm. Which of the following would be an AML red flag?

    A. She is an American author.

    B. She wired $100,000 but has not any investments in the past 6 months.

    C. She completes all of the fields in the required onboarding application.

    D. She claims he made his money from selling bestselling novels.

Question 109

Which of the following are not recommended procedures for filing STRs?

A. STRs should be centralized for review to ensure uniformity

B. STRs should be filed multiple times by each employee that comes across the activity.

C. STRs should only be filed after the suspicious actor has been notified.

D. STRs should only be filed after Legal has approved the filing.

Question 110

Which of the following is the most difficult regulatory challenge facing a foreign financial institution with a correspondent banking relationship in the US?

A. USA Patriot Act

B. Base Due Diligence Principles for Banks

C. FATF Guidance on Terrorist Financing

D. UN Security Council Resolution on Correspondent Banking

Question 111

What is the primary risk on concentration accounts?

    A. Additional recordkeeping is necessary and could be accidentally missed.

    B. None, concentration accounts cannot be accessed by clients.

    C. None, concentration accounts are a way to mitigate money laundering risk.

    D. Customer identification could be separated from the transaction amounts.

Question 112

What is Anti-Money Laundering International Database (AMLID)?

    A. A database at FATF of suspected money launderers and their organizations.

    B. A database in the International Money Laundering Information Network at the UN Office on Drugs and Crime that contains laws, regulations, and analysis, as well as contact information for law law enforcement in various jurisdictions.

    C. A database of laws and regulations pertaining to money laundering at the US Department of Justice.

    D. An FBI database of law enforcement contacts in other jurisdictions.

Question 113

What is a Currency Transaction Report (CTR)?

A. Report that documents the amount of currency transferred in and out of a bank in a given period.

B. Report that documents the amount of foreign currency transferred in and out of a bank in a given period.

C. Report that documents large currency transactions.

D. Report that documents suspicious transactions.

Question 114

IVTS is an abbreviation for...

A. Informal Value Taxation System

B. Informal Value Transfer System

C. International Value Taxation System

D. International Value Transfer System

Question 115

What are Nostro Accounts?

    A. Accounts for the clients of correspondence banking client.

    B. Accounts correspondent account for a foreign bank that provides a correspondent account for the domestic bank, a mutual correspondent bank.

    C. Accounts for correspondence bank that provides banking services to correspondence banking client.

    D. Accounts for correspondence banking client that receives banking services from a correspondence bank.

Question 116

Who are vital service providers?

    A. Accountants, architects, contractors, construction companies, civil engineers, telecommunications firms, and transportation companies

    B. Accountants, attorneys, doctors, nurses, EMTs, police officers, firefighters, telecommunications firms, and transportation companies

    C. Accountants, attorneys, government workers, telecommunications firms, and transportation companies

    D. Accountants, attorneys, broker-dealers, financial institutions, telecommunications firms, and transportation companies

Question 117

Which of the following are methods of money laundering at a casino?

A. Depositing illicit funds and gambling winnings at the casino in Las Vegas and then taking the money out in Atlantic City.

B. Depositing legitimate earnings from gambling into a prepaid credit card and sending the credit card to help terrorist.

C. Meeting with a dealer ahead of time to setup a strategy to fix the blackjack table.

D. Spending free reward points the casino has provided on the casino's hotel for lodging.

Question 118

Who is PEP with the most exposure?

A. Helen Zaltzman, Host of The Allusionist

B. Ira Glass, Host of This American Life

C. Kalpit Shah, Sr VP of compliance strategy at a regional bank

D. Malala Yousafzai, Nobel Peace Prize Winner

Question 119

You are a junior compliance officer at a large bank. You attend a AML conference and learn of a new requirement that will be implemented in six months. When you get back in the office, you should...

A. Get back to work and assume the senior compliance officers already know about the new requirement.

B. Check with the appropriate regulator to see if your bank could be given more time to meet the requirements.

C. Check with the appropriate senior compliance officer to see whether the bank is prepared for the new requirement.

D. Check with the appropriate senior compliance officer to see whether the bank is prepared to evade the new requirement.

Question 120

Jaap van Zweden is a new customer seeking life insurance products. Which of the following would an AML red flag?

A. He makes his wife his first beneficiary upon his death.

B. He makes full use of the free lookback period.

C. He takes a loss and ends the contract.

D. He reads the insurance contract carefully.

ANSWERS

1. _____

2. _____

3. _____

4. _____

5. _____

6. _____

7. _____

8. _____

9. _____

10. _____

11. _____

12. _____

13. _____

14. _____

15. _____

16. _____

17. _____

18. _____

19. _____

20. _____

21. _____

22. _____

23. _____

24. _____

25. _____

26. _____

27. _____

28. _____

29. _____

30. _____

31. _____

32. _____

33. _____

34. _____

35. _____

36. _____

37. _____

38. _____

39. _____

40. _____

41. _____

42. _____

43. _____

44. _____

45. _____

46. _____

47. _____

48. _____

49. _____

50. _____

51. _____

52. _____

53. _____

54. _____

55. _____

56. _____

57. _____

58. _____

59. _____

60. _____

61. _____

62. _____

63. _____

64. _____

65. _____

66. _____

67. _____

68. _____

69. _____

70. _____

71. _____

72. _____

73. _____

74. _____

75. _____

76. _____

77. _____

78. _____

79. _____

80. _____

81. _____

82. _____

83. _____

84. _____

85. _____

86. _____

87. _____

88. _____

89. _____

90. _____

91. _____

92. _____

93. _____

94. _____

95. _____

96. _____

97. _____

98. _____

99. _____

100. _____

101. _____

102. _____

103. _____

104. _____

105. _____

106. _____

107. _____

108. _____

109. _____

110. _____

111. _____

112. _____

113. _____

114. _____

115. _____

116. _____

117. _____

118. _____

119. _____

120. _____

ANSWERS

1.   C

2.   A,B,C

3.   A,B,C,D

4.   B

5.   C

6.   C

7.   D

8.   B

9.   D

10.   A

11.   B

12.   B

13.   D

14.   B

15.   D

16.   A,B,C,D

17.   B

18.   C

19. _____ A _____

20. _____ B _____

21. _____ A,B,C,D _____

22. _____ A,D _____

23. _____ B _____

24. _____ A,B,C,D _____

25. _____ B _____

26. _____ B _____

27. _____ A _____

28. _____ A _____

29. _____ A,D _____

30. _____ C _____

31. _____ B _____

32. _____ C _____

33. _____ C _____

34. _____ B _____

35. _____ C _____

36. _____ C _____

37. _____ A _____

38. _____ A,B,C _____

39. _____ A _____

40. _____ D _____

41. _____ D _____

42. _____ D _____

43. _____ C _____

44. _____ B _____

45. _____ A _____

46. _____ C _____

47. _____ A,B,C,D _____

48. _____ C _____

49. _____ B _____

50. _____ C _____

51. _____ B _____

52. _____ A _____

53. _____ D _____

54. _____ D _____

55. _____ A _____

56. _____ A _____

57. _____ C _____

58. _____ C _____

59. _____ D _____

60. _____ A,C,D _____

61. _____D_____

62. _____C_____

63. _____D_____

64. _____D_____

65. _____C_____

66. _____C_____

67. _____D_____

68. _____A,B,C,D_____

69. _____C_____

70. _____D_____

71. _____C_____

72. _____A,C,D_____

73. _____A,B,C,D_____

74. _____C_____

75. _____A_____

76. _____D_____

77. _____D_____

78. _____C_____

79. _____A_____

80. _____A_____

81. _____A_____

82. _____D_____

83. _____A,B,C_____

84. _____A,B_____

85. _____A_____

86. _____A_____

87. _____A,B,C,D_____

88. _____A_____

89. _____C_____

90. _____B_____

91. _____C_____

92. _____C_____

93. _____B_____

94. _____D_____

95. _____C_____

96. _____B_____

97. _____A_____

98. _____A_____

99. _____A_____

100. _____D_____

101. _____A_____

102. _____A_____

103. _____ C _____

104. _____ D _____

105. _____ A _____

106. _____ D _____

107. _____ A,B,C _____

108. _____ B _____

109. _____ B,C,D _____

110. _____ A _____

111. _____ A,D _____

112. _____ B _____

113. _____ C _____

114. _____ B _____

115. _____ B _____

116. _____ D _____

117. _____ A _____

118. _____ D _____

119. _____ C _____

120. _____ B,C _____

M. C. Maltempo

M. C. Maltempo is a principal consultant at Ventures of MJ LLC. He has been involved in the investigations of some of the largest cases in history. Early in his career, he helped investigate auditors' malpractice in advising the executives of Adelphia Communications. He then later helped JPMorgan's internal investigation team into the London Whale trades. He is a Certified Anti-Money Laundering Specialist (CAMS) and a Certified Fraud Examiner (CFE). He holds an MBA from Thunderbird School of Global Management.